I0801734

THE GHOSTLY TALES OF THE RIO GRANDE VALLEY

Published by Arcadia Children's Books
A Division of Arcadia Publishing
Charleston, SC
www.arcadiapublishing.com

Copyright © 2023 by Arcadia Children's Books
All rights reserved

Spooky America is a trademark of Arcadia Publishing, Inc.

First published 2023

Manufactured in the United States

ISBN 978-1-4671-9737-3

Library of Congress Control Number: 2023937850

Notice: The information in this book is true and complete to the best of our knowledge. It is offered without guarantee on the part of the author or Arcadia Publishing. The author and Arcadia Publishing disclaim all liability in connection with the use of this book.

All rights reserved. No part of this book may be reproduced or transmitted in any form whatsoever without prior written permission from the publisher except in the case of brief quotations embodied in critical articles and reviews.

Images used courtesy of Shutterstock.com.

Spooky America

The Ghostly Tales of The Rio Grande Valley

KAREN EMILY MILLER

Adapted from *Ghosts of the Rio Grande Valley* by David Bowles

arcadia CHILDREN'S BOOKS

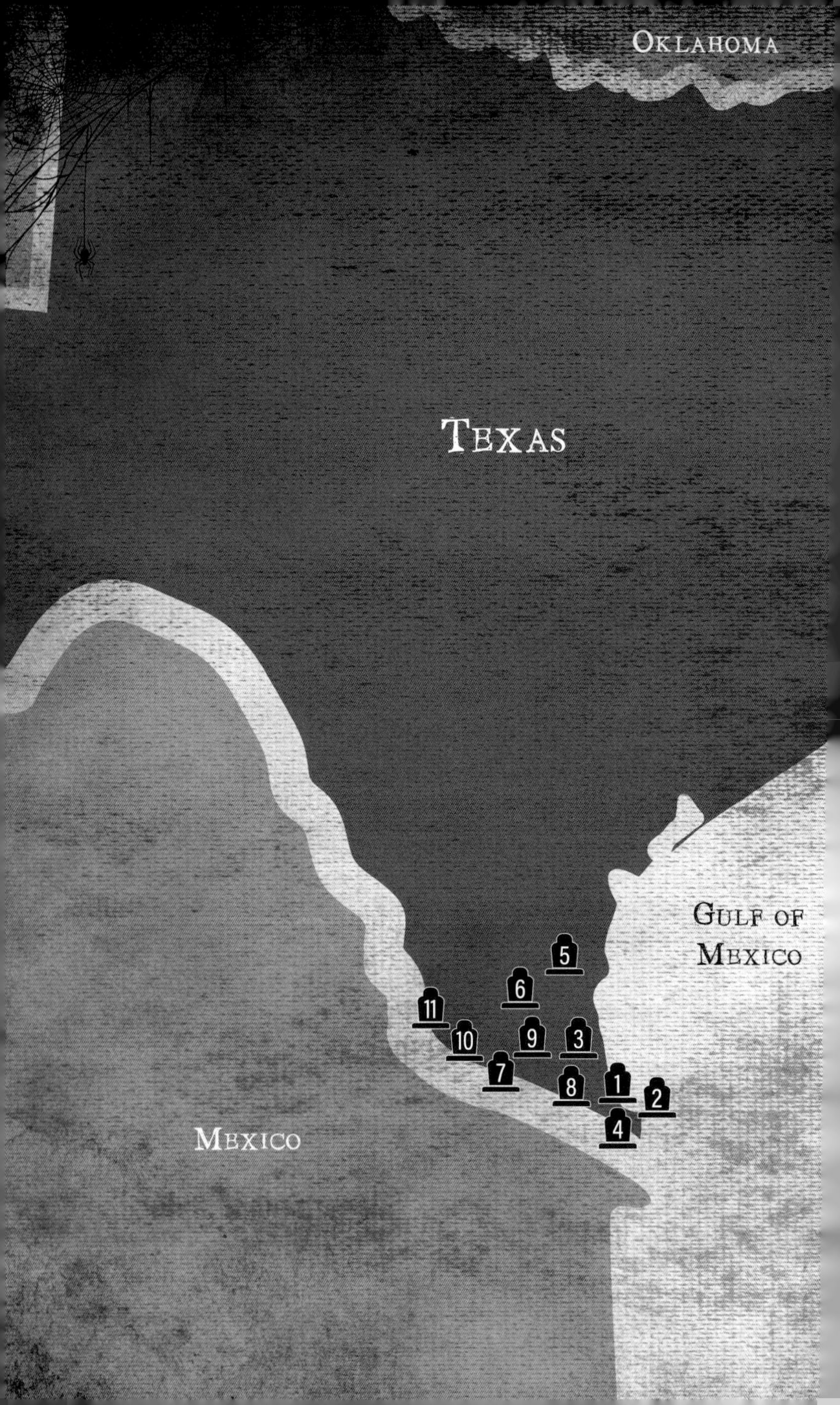
Oklahoma
Texas
Gulf of
Mexico
Mexico
1
2
3
4
5
6
7
8
9
10
11

Table of Contents & Map Key

Welcome to the Spooky Rio Grande Valley!

The Rio Grande Valley will surprise you. You expect to see ranches with acres stretching to the horizon. You've heard about the sky that never ends. You know stories about the Texas Rangers and the bandits.

But there's so much more than that. Here, you'll swim in oxbow lakes. You might see wild cats like ocelots or jaguarundis. You might feel a surge of panic when you almost step on a six-inch-long horned lizard. But you'll never be bored.

The people who settled this land were tough. The kind of people who can weather harsh winters, brutally hot summers, and dangerous animals. It's no wonder that the ghosts are tough, too. Once they've become attached to a place, they don't leave. In the Rio Grande Valley, children hear tales of demons, witches, monsters, and "*cucuys*"—mythical ghost-monsters said to roam the dark in search of their next victim. A ghost might be

kindly, like Mr. Shary who dances with his wife in the sky, or sad, like those freedom seekers caught forever in an underground tunnel. Or it could be La Llorona who drowns children, or the Tampacua warriors, fated to fight Texas Rangers again and again, forever.

When you visit the Rio Grande Valley, you'll find four counties full of ghosts waiting to meet you. But watch out! They might like you so much . . . they'll never let you go.

CHAPTER 1

Stanolin Road

You've never minded being an only child, except for road trips where there's no Wi-Fi. That's when you wish you had a brother or sister to compete against in a game of spotting out-of-state license plates. You imagine that if you were really bored, you could tease them. But tonight, with no Wi-Fi signal and no siblings, you're stuck.

Your mom suggests counting cows. She reminds you that since you are in South Texas, you should spot hundreds of them by the time you get to the hotel. Your dad tries to find Farm Road 511 because there are rumors of ghost cows.

When your parents first suggested a trip that would make everybody happy, you'd felt excited. During the day, Mom and Dad would go birding since South Texas is famous for birds that aren't seen anywhere else in the United States. Then in the evening, they'd drive you around to investigate ghostly places because you really like spooky stuff.

But now, you've been driving for what feels like forever. It's too dark to see anything. Dad announces you're lost. You wonder who will lose their temper first. You are all tired.

Suddenly, your dad hits the brakes and brings the car to a screeching halt. You swivel around to see what could have made him risk your lives.

All you see is a small white cross with plastic flowers at its base. You've seen crosses like that before. They are reminders that someone died in a car crash in that very spot. Your mom says that they are a reminder to slow down so you won't crash, too.

"That's not why I stopped," your dad says. He sounds a little worried. "I saw someone, just beyond the cross. "Look." He points into the darkness. "He's coming toward us."

Your dad's right, you realize. A man, or what *looks* like a man, is limping slowly toward your car. The sight of him getting closer makes your pulse pick up.

"Maybe he needs help," your dad says and clicks open his seat belt.

You yell, "Stop!" What is he doing? Doesn't your dad see what you see? And your whole life, haven't your parents been telling you not to talk to strangers?

The moonlight has just peeked out from behind the clouds, so you can see the man more clearly. Is it a trick of the light, or do the features on his face seem to be *sliding* back and forth?

"Can we go back to the hotel?" you beg your dad. "*Please?*"

Maybe because you were being polite, or maybe because your dad's finally come to his senses, but he clicks his seatbelt back on. He locks the doors.

You breathe a sigh of relief. But the man is still coming closer. You see him raise his hand. It's as if he's waving hello. He grins.

Something about that grin sends shivers down your spine. You sink down into the pillows and blankets you had made into a makeshift bed in the backseat.

The man smiles and limps closer. That's when you realize he doesn't have teeth—or even a mouth! His face puckers into a gaping hole above his chin. How is that even possible?

Your dad must be wondering the exact same thing, because half a second later, he guns the motor. You don't think any of you even dare to look back until you reach the city lights.

Ghost Number 1: *check*.

CHAPTER 2

Port Isabel Lighthouse

You've been on many car trips with your parents. They love history and nature. You love ghosts. Luckily, everywhere you've gone has something for each of you. So, when you pull up to the Port Isabel Lighthouse, a historic lighthouse, you figure you're there for *you*. The lighthouse, now a museum, must have lots of ghosts. Spirits from dead sailors and travelers. Maybe a lighthouse keeper who tripped down the spiral staircase?

Your mom and dad say you are half right. Yes, there will be a paranormal experience, but it won't be inside the lighthouse. You'll have to wait until evening to see it, so your mom suggests you take the museum tour inside while you wait for the dark.

You don't mind. Knowing the story behind the lighthouse might make meeting its ghosts more exciting.

"This lighthouse saved many lives," says the museum guide.

You roll your eyes. You'd hoped this would be more stimulating. Everyone knows lighthouses save lives.

"At night or in storms," the guide continues, "ships couldn't see the breakers—the rocks along the shore. Many of the ships crashed into the rocks and sunk. So, in the 1800s, a lighthouse was built. It wasn't as big as most. It was only seventy-five steps high, but it lit the bay well enough for ships to sail into port safely."

By this time, you've climbed up to the lighthouse lamp.

"The original light was an oil lamp with three wicks," the guide says. "Now it's a mercury vapor light." The guide points to the green, gold, and chartreuse lights and demonstrates all their flashing patterns. "In 1905, the lighthouse was decommissioned. There wasn't enough water traffic to make it worthwhile. Trains and semitrucks took over most of the shipping traffic."

You yawn. When are you getting to the ghosts?

"That didn't stop the lighthouse from saving lives. Even though ships no longer used it, the lighthouse continued to help. Its angel never stopped coming."

You look around the tower. An angel? *That's* interesting.

"The lighthouse had been a place of safety, not just from storms. During the Mexican–American

War, and then the Civil War, soldiers from both sides took refuge here. At times, it was one side who camped at the base, other times, it was the opposite. When cholera and yellow fever hit, the lighthouse became a makeshift hospital." He explains that for generations, people claim to have seen ghostly figures wandering around the lighthouse—often at dusk, after the sun's gone down. "Some people think they might be the ghost of Civil War soldiers. Or the restless spirits of those who died from cholera. People who never received a proper burial."

"What do you think?" you ask.

The guide pauses. "I think there are a lot of things about this place we can't explain."

For a moment, you look up at the lighthouse. You try to imagine all the souls who suffered here, and all the ghosts who likely now call this place home. It's no wonder some of them never left, you think. Maybe all that fear, sadness, and even anger have tied them here.

The guide goes on to say that the first sign there was something supernatural about the lighthouse came after a ship landed safely, even though the seas were rough and the skies black. The sailor in the crow's nest saw a giant angel hovering over the lighthouse. Her glow was so bright, it lit a safe passage through the choppy, dark waters.

The story about the angel spread. According to locals, the angel not only illuminated the night, but it also whispered warnings and advice to those who would listen. A young man claimed he heard the angel telling him to cancel a trip to Mexico City. His fiancée had been looking forward to seeing the city of her ancestors. But he convinced her to change their destination to Acapulco. It was a city in the homeland, too, he argued. The morning after they arrived in Acapulco, they felt their bed move and shake. A massive earthquake had struck Mexico, and over five thousand people in Mexico City died.

The guide leads your group back outside. A

light rain is falling. Your mom is ready to get back into the car. "Wait," the guide says. He motions for you to look up. "Watch and you'll understand why people see the angel."

You glance at the sky. As you watch storm clouds swirl high above, strong winds buffet the lighthouse. They make two windy whirls alongside the top of the tower, gathering droplets of rain as they spin. "*Wow*," you whisper. The sight is mesmerizing. The wind and rain appear to dance together around the lamp, bending the rays of light into what looks like a giant halo that floats above the cupola.

"It looks like angel wings," your dad marvels.

The wind whistles and moans, as if in reply.

For a second, it almost seems like the wind is speaking to *you*.

Mom touches your shoulder. "Let's get back in the car and dry off," she says.

You hesitate. You just heard something you can't explain—you're *certain* of it. The wind, repeating itself over and over, whispers a word that sounds like "*Union.*" You look at your parents. They don't seem to have heard it.

Union as in . . . Union solider? you wonder. Is this a Civil War ghost trying to talk to you?

You start to open the car door but don't climb in. Then, suddenly, you hear something else, words that are almost lost in the wind. This voice is clear, melodious, and slow. "Don't end up like me."

You crack a puzzled smile. A Civil War ghost with a sense of humor?

The guide was right. The lighthouse *had* saved lives. If not from shining a light in the darkness and keeping countless ships safe, then from its angel. Whether the angel is a paranormal occurrence or a just a weather phenomenon doesn't really matter. Either way, it's nice to imagine that someone—or some*thing*—was looking out for those who come for a visit.

CHAPTER 3

The Weeping Woman, La Llorona

You thought you knew all about La Llorona, a spirit in Mexican and Latin American folklore who cries as she haunts rivers and waterways in search of her lost children. There are lots of TV shows, movies, and documentaries about the Weeping Woman. What you don't know is how the story began. Luckily, this morning, your mom and dad take you to a museum with a guide who likes to talk. Maybe it's because you're the only ones in her tour group, but she talks much longer than the thirty minutes scheduled.

"You might think you know all about the Weeping Woman," she says mysteriously. "But you don't. Did you know her story begins before time, when the Aztec gods ruled the world?"

She talks about how the Aztec gods were militaristic, at times cruel, and always fiercely protective of their people. When mankind appeared, the gods made sure people followed their rules to keep the universe working. Making sure the sun rose and set every day was vital. It took more than the gods to keep the sun safe from the underworld demons. If a woman died in childbirth, she joined the ranks of divine women. It was her honor, until the end of time, to guard the sun as it descended into the underworld each night. That was when evil spirits tried to destroy the sun. The divine women stopped them.

However, the nature of a divine woman was as fearful as the demons of the underworld. She was single-minded. She would destroy anything that might stop the sun from rising. Anyone could be taken as a threat. An unlucky child or a wandering tourist might draw her attention and make her think the sun was in danger. By the time the divine woman was finished with them, they'd be driven insane.

"Some said the Weeping Woman was the goddess Cihuacōātl, who lived under Lake Texcoco in Mexico," the guide explains. "She was said to rise from the lake whenever she felt the people of Mexico were threatened. She would call, "Where should I hide my children? Run!" to anyone who would listen."

Your guide looks at her watch, decides she has time for one more tale, then says she has a different origin story for the Weeping Woman and that this one is her favorite.

"Ghosts are tied to the place where they lived their most intense experience. Sometimes it is happy, sometimes sad, sometimes frightening."

There was a woman in Mexico's history whom many considered treacherous. Her name was La Malinche, and she helped the Spanish conquistador Cortés defeat the Aztecs. She spoke many languages, including Spanish, so she could tell Cortés what people were really thinking when they spoke. Because of her, Cortés received a thorough understanding of the Aztecs and other tribes. Many blamed her for the Aztec defeat.

"Why would she betray her own people? There might be no emotion stronger than revenge to make someone do such a thing. La Malinche had

reason to hate the Aztecs, even though she was one of them. She had been sold into slavery by her own family. While enslaved, she learned the languages of the tribes of the Aztec Empire. She might also have learned that knowledge is power. With her gift of languages, she gained tremendous power."

Your mom asks, "Did she ever regret what she had done?"

"Perhaps. The Weeping Woman walks because she can't rid herself of pain. Is it the pain of betraying her people? Or is it the pain of committing an act so terrible, that of killing her children, that it can never be forgiven? Is that why the Weeping Woman walks along the lake shores? Why are there so many weeping women? No one knows."

Your dad asks her if there is a place where you might see the Weeping Woman. The guide sends you to the lake in the middle of town. Right away, you notice there's a trail that runs alongside the lake. It's short, just long enough to stretch your legs, but not long enough for you to get tired out. There's also a shelter where you can set up your camp chairs and stay out of the afternoon sun.

To your surprise, you aren't the only ones waiting to see her. A lady asks your parents if she can join you, and of course, they say yes. Your dad, always the gentleman, tells you to give the lady your chair.

She asks, "Are you waiting to see La Llorona?"

Your parents nod and ask if she knows any ghost stories about her.

You really wish they hadn't asked that. The last thing you want right now is to get stuck listening to a stranger's story, especially when there's no guarantee it's going to be a good one. Also, you've heard so many stories about La Llorona today that you doubt she's going to tell you anything new.

The lady begins: "In the valley, there are weeping women anywhere there is a lake or river."

Your ears perk up. *Any* lake or river? Okay, okay. Maybe you *will* learn something new.

"Look there." She points to the other side of the lake. "Women used to gather at the lakeshore to wash clothes for their families. One day, a Texas Ranger named Lawrence was out for a walk. He noticed Dafne right away. She was the most beautiful woman he'd ever seen. It was love at first sight for him, but Dafne needed convincing. Lawrence was a Texas Ranger, after all, and they were known to be unfair—even cruel—to the locals."

"Did he ever convince her?" you ask.

The lady nods. "It took Lawrence months to convince Dafne and her family that he was worthy enough for her to marry. Finally, they agreed. The Ranger said he was rich, and he certainly was charming. What more could a poor family ask for?"

Uh oh. You can't help feeling like this story is about to take a dark turn.

"Time passed," she says. "Dafne and Lawrence had two boys and seemed happy. But when the relations between the United States and Mexico soured, so did their marriage. Lawrence turned his back on Dafne and her family. He even killed her brother in a skirmish between the Rangers and the locals."

"Oh no," your mom says. "What about the children?"

"He left them," the lady replies. "Dafne wept until she had no more tears. Eventually, though, anger took over her grief. In Dafne's world, there was only one way to punish Lawrence, and that was to take away the thing that mattered *most* to him: their children. That night, she put the washing and the boys on top of the family donkey. Calmly, quietly, she led the boys to the river. All she could think of was hurting the man who broke her heart. In a trance, she led the donkey into the deep water."

You already know how this story ends, but it's no less heartbreaking.

"She drowned the boys," the lady says somberly. "And then herself. People say that she wanted to take herself and her children to a place where they could never feel pain. But Dafne's plan didn't work. To this day, she suffers. She can't leave her grief behind."

"How terribly tragic," your mom says.

"She *did*, however, get her wish to punish Lawrence," the lady interjects. "It's said that Lawrence had second thoughts about leaving his family just before he boarded the train. But at the last second, he felt a pain so deep that it was almost as if his heart were being ripped out. He jumped on a horse and raced home, but he was too late. He found the house empty, the donkey gone. He knew right away where Dafne had taken the children. He found their bodies floating in the water." The lady pauses for a moment, as if out of respect for the dead. "The boys were given a proper burial," she says. "But Dafne was not. They never found her body."

At those words, a chill sweeps over you. You can feel the lady studying all your faces. You think she's checking to see if her story scared you.

It did.

But the story's not over yet.

"How did the family go on?" your dad asks.

"Dafne's sisters took over doing laundry for others," the lady replies. "Something had to be done to support the family. One evening, the two youngest nieces wandered away as the older ones worked. They threw rocks into the water and chased each other. They were so involved in their

play that they didn't notice the arrival of a strange woman. She was an odd sort; someone they didn't recognize. Drenched, covered in mud, she blocked their way to the shore.

"*Where are they*?" the woman cried. "*Where are my children*?" Before the girls could answer, she pulled them down to the lake's bottom."

You gasp. You didn't think it was possible for this story to get any sadder—but it has!

That's when the lady looks at you. "How old are you, my dear? You're just a child, aren't you?"

You look back at her, a little caught off guard by her question. Why does she care how old you are? Before you can answer, you notice tiny puddles of water under her chair.

Suddenly, you realize how pale her face is, even partially hidden below a big, wide-brimmed sun hat. In fact, her skin is *so* pale, it almost seems transparent . . . as if you are looking at her underwater.

The lady's eyes lock on yours once more, and then she blinks. When she opens her eyes again, they have changed from faded blue to *black pools*.

A millisecond later, you are sprinting to your car. Luckily, your parents parked by the shelter, so you're inside with the doors locked lightning fast. You have a feeling you could've outrun the old lady, even if she *was* La Llorona.

You reach into your backpack and grab bug spray. That should stop her.

Outside, you hear your mom and dad calling you. Reluctantly, you unlock the doors, climb out, and head to the shelter, bug spray at attention, just in case.

"Where did she go?" you ask your parents when you reach them.

Your mom and dad look confused. "We wanted to ask you the same question. It embarrassed us, the way you ran off. We turned to apologize, but the lady was gone . . . disappeared."

You glance over to where you'd all been sitting just a few minutes ago. Yep, she's gone. The only way to prove she was ever sitting there was the chair. It's dripping with muddy lake water.

CHAPTER 4

The Colonial Hotel

As you arrive at the Colonial Hotel, you wonder if your parents are right. Was this the site of some mysterious burials? Is that why it's rumored to be haunted? Your parents know a lot about history. It's likely that they are right.

Your mom reads aloud from a history book about the Rio Grande Valley, summarizing as she goes. She knows you and your dad only like hearing highlights, not the whole text.

"The lower Rio Grande Valley has long been the home to the Lipan Apache. They lived on the land for generations. It wasn't always peaceful. There were wars between neighboring people, and lives were lost. All of them, however, followed codes of honor when it came to burying the dead.

The traditions of honor ended with the Spanish. They had heard stories about cities of gold and wanted the fame that came with conquering a new world. Being devout Catholics of the time, they felt it was their duty to baptize everyone. It was God, gold, and glory that drove them. What did they care about the rituals of the Native Americans?

The Spanish fired their muskets in battle and fought with the local people. But they didn't stop to give their dead opponents proper burials. Little did they know how important that ritual was.

The Lipan Apache believed that when people die, their earthly bodies crumble into dust. But their spirits live on. These ghosts were dangerous unless they arose from a baby, a child, or an elderly person. An unburied ghost was angry—so angry it would pledge to drive whomever it encountered into madness so terrible, the victim could not endure it.

The ghost sickness, the spirit's revenge, crept into one's dreams. The ghost knew, down to the smallest detail, all the events that had horrified the victims during their lives.

So, the Lipan Apache took great care in burying people when they died. They made certain the body was buried with the head facing east. They waved branches of smoking sage during the ceremony. Sometimes, they would move camp after the burial. No one wanted to be near the dead.

If, however, the burial wasn't done correctly, the ghost was condemned to wander the earth forever, giving ghost sickness to anyone it encountered.

"That would be one scary ghost," you agree. Still, you're excited. The Colonial Hotel was known to be home to a number of angry spirits. Maybe you'll see one!

A porter grabs your suitcases and tells you to follow him. Your parents ask for the most haunted room in the hotel, which is room 101. As he shuts the hotel door behind him, the clerk smiles. "Sleep well," he says. "Your parents would do well to keep their eyes open all night."

Did he cackle after he said that? What kind of night will you have?

The rollaway bed creaks as you sit down. You look around the room. Not fancy, but clean. That's all you ask for when you travel. Besides, fancy hotels are less likely to house a ghost.

Your mom and dad announce they are going to get a Piccadilly shaved ice (a sweet cherry syrup and pickle juice snow cone), just like the one you finished moments ago. You'll admit you weren't so sure about that flavor combination at first, but turns out, those things are surprisingly tasty.

"We'll be back by supper," your dad says. "You have nothing to worry about. That porter must like scaring the guests."

"Besides," your mom adds. "The ghost guide said the very old, like the clerk, and young, like you, have nothing to fear from the spirits. The young haven't had time to commit terrible deeds, and as for the old, the ghosts don't want to waste their energy on them. The old will be in the underworld soon enough."

You wave them away to work on a questionnaire for any ghosts you might meet. You write down the questions. "Why are you no longer on earth? How did you die? Why won't you leave?" You must be sleepier than you thought because you doze off with your notebook and pencil on your lap.

You wake to voices whispering above, below, and even beside you. There are so many ghosts gabbling, you can't distinguish who is talking to you! Is that your grandfather's voice? Maybe it's your great aunt, the one you only met once. Some voices you don't recognize. Their words, though, you understand. You hope you never hear them again.

"Come child. Come to us. We're waiting for you."

You crack open your eyes, hoping whatever is in the room won't see that you are awake. At first, gentle tugs pull at you from under the sheets. Then wriggling fingers push their way through and grab your feet.

You scream just as your mom and dad come through the door. It's only after they check you, head to toe, that they declare you had a nightmare.

You settle back in for the night. You wait for your parents' familiar snorts and snores to begin. You've almost fallen asleep when your mom shrieks.

"There's something under the bed! It grabbed me and tried to pull me through the mattress!"

Your dad groans like he does when one of you hears something scary. But he gets up and crouches down to look under the bed just in case. You wait for him to laugh and say the only thing under the bed is dust bunnies. He doesn't laugh. He yells.

You can't believe what you see at first. Two

pale hands shoot out from under the bed and grab him by his ankles. Your dad is strong, but tonight he doesn't seem like it. His feet, then his legs disappear under the bed. You and your mom each grab one of his arms and pull. It feels as if he is stuck in muck, even quicksand! Finally, you pull him out.

Your mom switches on the lamp while your dad, panting, collapses on the bed.

"It was dark," he says, "almost as if all the light in the world had been sucked away. It seemed like the dark was trying to pull me inside it."

That isn't the end of it.

Thump! Thump!

Heartbreaking moans and pitiful cries whirl out from under their bed. So you all jump on *your* bed. A second later, a form—more like a headless, limbless corpse than a human—worms its way from under the bed. It seems to sniff around looking for you and your parents.

"A human bundle ghost," your dad says. "They'd

appear before Aztec warriors. If the men ran away, they were condemned as cowards for the rest of their life."

Your mom grabs your dad's hand and whispers, "No, not the baby ghost!" From the corner of the room toddles what some might call a baby, but it doesn't look like any baby you've ever seen. The baby ghost is followed a woman. At least you think it's a woman. Its face has been shot off by a cannon.

"Run!" your dad says.

You kick away a chair so that you have a clear path to the door. As fast as you are, you're no match for the next spirit. A warrior with an owl perched on his shoulder waits for you by the hotel door. The owl's yellow eyes look at you but never blink. Blood drips from its beak. Blood drips from the warrior's lips.

The sight makes you all scream, but you don't care. Who cares if the spirits think you are cowardly?

You run through the ghost warrior and the ghost bird. As you push your way through, you feel a cold so icy, it grabs and tries to hold you. You feel for the doorknob, find it, and wrench it open.

You tumble out of room 101 and into the hall. The night manager is there in seconds, pulling you up and checking for bruises.

"I heard screaming!" he says. "Didn't the desk clerk warn you?"

You explain that he said it was haunted—not deadly! You wait outside while someone gathers your things so you can spend the rest of the night in another room. But even in a different room, you barely get any sleep. You're too wired from your epic ghost aventure.

Still, you grab your pen and notebook and jot a note to yourself: The next stop should be scary, yes. But life-threatening?

No, thanks!

CHAPTER 5

The Devil's Lagoon

We're getting close!" your dad says. "Look, it's an oxbow lake."

You're not sure why your parents seem so excited. "It's just a lake. Nobody else is even here."

"That's because it's private property," your mom explains. "It's part of a ranch. We had to get permission to visit. They don't like people trespassing."

You glance out the window, feeling bored. You can think of better places to visit. Almost anything would be better than driving along a rutted road on a dusty evening in South Texas.

"Trust us," your mom chimes in. "This is not an ordinary lake. It started off as a branch of the Rio Grande River. When nature and time close off the branch, they leave behind a U-shaped lake. Some people say it looks like yokes oxen wear."

"So that's why it's called an oxbow lake," you answer, sighing. "I get it."

Your dad laughs. "That's right. But this lake has another name. It's called the Devil's Lagoon."

Devil's Lagoon? You perk up a little in your seat. Now THAT sounds interesting.

"While Dad and I are looking for the green jays, you can sit by the lake and look for the phantom coach," your mom says.

Phantom coach? Okay, this might be more fun than you thought.

Your dad begins the story. "It starts like most fairy tales. The boy and girl marry and live happily ever after, but sadly, not the way they'd hoped."

He goes on to say that at first, when the young couple asked their parents for permission to marry, both families celebrated. For weeks, the families cooked, baked, and cleaned their homes. They used sprays of cedar oleander to freshen the air and laid quilts and mattresses out in the sun. A calf slowly roasted, and hens were prepared, ready to bake. What a happy day it would be!

The day of the wedding was perfect. The South Texas sky stretched to the horizon. It was so clear, you could see the weather coming. No storms, just

blue skies. After the ceremony at church, the bride and groom took seats of honor in the hired coach. Their parents happily climbed in, too. The rest of the family and friends piled into wagons and carriages and followed the bridal coach. Dancing, eating, a few sips of tequila . . . it would be a night to remember!

Perhaps everyone was too excited to notice when the coach veered off the main road onto a road damaged with potholes. By the time the couple could no longer ignore the bone-rattling bumps and dusty clouds, it was too late to turn back. They called out to the coachman. "Where are you taking us?"

"Nothing to worry about it," he replied. "This is a shortcut to the ranch."

The parents were surprised at the change in direction. They raised their eyebrows and nudged each other but said nothing. Perhaps it was time for the young couple to begin making their own decisions.

The sun was setting when the coachman called, "There it is! The bridge. We'll be at the ranch in no time!"

The passengers looked out the windows. There was a bridge. It did cross over a deep lagoon near the ranch. But it was so old and weather-beaten, it didn't look like it could hold anything heavier than a man.

"Slow down!" the groom called to the driver.

The coachman ignored him. He cracked his whip and spurred the horses to run.

Halfway across the bridge, the bridal party heard a splintering crack followed by a high-pitched rip as the bridge collapsed and split open. The carriage plunged into the lagoon's dark waters. So did the horses, the families, and the grinning coachman. They were never seen again.

"Whoa!" you exclaim. "What happened? Why did the bridge break?"

"Nobody knows," your mom says. "But some people believe that on certain nights, especially in the glow of the autumn moon, you can still hear the terrifying crack of the coachman's angry whip and the screams of his passengers. They say his demon spirit drives his phantom horses and carriage out of the lagoon, carrying the ghosts of the dead back to the living world of the Rio Grande Valley."

"*Cool*," you whisper. "Now THAT'S something I'd like to see."

Your mom frowns. "I'm not so sure about that."

"Why not?" you ask.

"Well," she replies, "they say not everyone who sees this demon ghost is lucky enough to escape alive." She motions to the sky, which is growing darker by the second. "Do you think we should test that theory?"

You glance out the window, thinking about the name *Devil's Lagoon*. It doesn't *look* dangerous. It's just a regular old lake surrounded by marshes.

Isn't it?

But the longer you stare, the more you think you see a strange movement in the water. A ripple, like there might be more than meets the eye about this place after all.

"Maybe not," you finally agree.

As your car pulls away, you turn toward the lake one last time. You wonder what secrets it holds. And exactly what—or *who*—may be lurking beneath its dark, shimmery surface.

CHAPTER 6

The Old Hidalgo County Jail

It's not surprising that the Hidalgo County Jail is haunted. After all, death lived there.

That's why your family signed up for the night tour. It's more likely you'll see a ghost at night. Plus, the brochure promises a paranormal experience. So you're pretty much guaranteed to see something spooky.

That is, if you don't run away screaming first.

Unlike most tours, this one is quiet, almost silent. Everyone seems a bit nervous. There is no moon, no shining stars. And you're heading for the gallows.

An actor dressed like an old-time sheriff begins the tour on the first floor. "This is a good place to start," he says. "No one died here, so you have time to prepare yourself for what's up there." He points to the ceiling. "That's where the ghosts are."

He waves his hands around the courtroom. "This is where people were accused and sentenced for crimes."

You don't feel any cold spots or hear anything suspicious. You relax.

Then, you climb the steps to the cells. You wait so you can be at the end of the line. You don't want anyone fainting on you.

That's when you feel a blanket of cold settling over you.

"This is where the prisoners were held," the guide says.

You stop in front of one of the cells. He opens the door so you can peek inside. How would it feel to be trapped inside a cell no bigger than a bathroom? You think of the people who were locked inside here. Not just poachers and wrongly accused men and women, but also robbers and murderers.

The guide stops in front of a steel door. "And *this* is where they'd meet their end."

Your mom raises her hand. "I thought only one prisoner was executed here."

The guide frowns. "I will get to that after I show you the gallows."

He leads you to the hanging room. It's crammed between jail cells. You feel an intense heaviness the moment you step inside. What if you were sitting in your cell and heard the drop of a body?

"We don't usually show people this," the guide explains. "It's too creepy for some of our guests. It's a tower room, two stories tall so it can hold high gallows."

You remember reading about high gallows. In standard gallows, the accused was hanged by putting a noose around his neck and dropping him a few feet. In high gallows, there was a long drop. You imagine the hanging platform with its crossbeam and noose and shiver.

Talk about creepy!

"There was only prisoner who died on these gallows," the guide says. "The rest were sent to the state penitentiary. It was only one man, but he was so evil, we think he tainted the whole jail."

He goes on to explain the man was named Ortiz. He and a friend attacked a local couple as they returned home after a day of doing errands. They killed the husband, but the wife escaped. With her testimony, Ortiz and his friend were found guilty and sentenced to death by hanging. Ortiz's friend escaped to Mexico, never to be captured.

A few days before the hanging, Ortiz was moved to the maximum-security cell. The thick steel door stood between him and possible escape. No one wanted to take any chances.

As time drew near for the execution, the jailers offered Ortiz time to confess his sins to a priest. They hoped he'd confess and show regret for what he had done.

Ortiz, though, laughed at the offer. When it was time for the executioners to slip a bag over his head, he pulled it off. He said he wanted to look at the people who had come to witness his hanging. He was right in thinking many would come to see him die. Hundreds had come, by the wagonload, horseback, and on foot.

When the executioners warned him that his

eyes would pop at the moment of death, Ortiz changed his mind. He wanted to die as a man of fear, not a man to be laughed at.

His last words were chilling.

He was reported to have said, "My body might be gone, but I'm going to cling to this world like a tick."

The guide lets you take turns standing in the death watch cell. It's only for a minute or two, but long enough for the chill to intensify. It's almost as if you're encased in ice. But that's when you notice a strange sound. Are someone's teeth chattering? No, it doesn't sound like teeth clacking together. It's the rattling of chains followed by a metallic clank. Was that the sound a lever made when it released the trap door? You look around the group. Judging by the confused faces you see all around, you think everyone heard it.

After the tour, everyone files out of the jail. You notice that the whole group is extra quiet. Maybe because they want to hear that jangle of chains again. Or maybe . . . they just don't want to get on Ortiz's bad side. Either way, no one lingers in the parking lot.

Hearing about the death of a killer was awful. How much worse would it be if you had seen him, too?

You don't think anyone wanted to find out.

CHAPTER 7

Casa de Palmas

A morning all to yourself! This time your mom and dad are off looking for buff-bellied hummingbirds. You settle yourself in the lobby with your notebooks. Maybe it's a slow day for business, because the clerk comes out from behind the front desk to talk to you. He grabs a coffee and drops down in a nearby chair.

"You're a ghost hunter?" he asks.

You look at your notebooks and books piled next to you. *Ghosts of the Rio Grande Valley, Ghosthunter Guide, Texas Haunts*. "Yep," you say. "Does the hotel have any?"

"We have at least three ghosts, maybe four." He calls over a kid about your age who is playing on a laptop. "This is my nephew. He's staying with me for the weekend. I like to keep him busy. David, show him the ghosts, please."

You feel a little sorry for the kid. You wouldn't want to spend your free time doing errands for your uncle. If some of his chores meant meeting ghosts, though, maybe it wouldn't be so bad after all.

David leads you out of the lobby and down into the basement. "I don't know if we'll see her," he says. "It's daytime and she usually appears at night."

You poke around empty rooms of boxes, extra chairs, and tables. There's dust but no ghosts.

"She's the oldest ghost we have. My uncle says she peeks her head into all the corners, almost as if she's looking for something."

You peek into corners, too, but don't see anything. "Oh well," you say. "Guess we're not going to see her. Thanks, anyway."

David asks, "Can you come back at midnight?"

You nod excitedly.

The day drags by and so does the evening. At midnight, you grab your backpack. You and your parents head to the lobby. "Where's David?" you ask the clerk when you get to the desk.

"Too late for him to stay up," the clerk says. "School tomorrow. No problem, though. I'll take you."

He leads you up the stairwell to the third floor. You tiptoe, not wanting to wake other guests. Maybe you're *too* quiet, though, because you don't meet the ghosts of the third floor. Not even a whisper of anything spooky. You can't help feeling disappointed. You've waited all day to see them, but it's just another no-show. You've literally been *ghosted* by the ghosts!

Your mom says she's glad the ghosts are gone for the night. She's heard that the ladies are terrifying and try to trap you in the stairwell. She says if you peer under their heavy black veils, you can see skin that looks like burnt charcoal.

Your dad can tell you're disappointed. "What about the ghost of Miss Roxy?" he asks the clerk. "Wasn't she a secretary who worked for the hotel? Isn't she supposed to be on the third floor?'

"That's where she's said to have had her office." The clerk pulls out a key card, inserts it into a lock, and lets you look inside. Nothing. Just an ordinary hotel room.

You sigh. So much for staying in a haunted hotel. The clerk must notice your disappointment, because when you return to the lobby a few minutes later, he gets you hot chocolate with a dash of red pepper and some sweet churros. "The original hotel burned to the ground," he explains. "People say the ladies were caught in the fire. Now their ghosts roam the halls. I'm sorry you didn't see them." He leans forward and asks, "Would you believe we have ghosts if it appeared in a police report? It happened a few years ago. One of the hotel managers saw movement in one of our towers. You've noticed them, I'm sure. Our two towers are distinctive. No other hotel here has them."

It's true, you think. The Casa de Palmas is very pretty. With its red tile twin-towers, palm-fronded patio, and cool breezes that blow in from the Gulf, you can see why anyone would want to visit—even ghosts.

"At first," he says, "he thought he had imagined seeing someone. He squinted, changed position, and still saw something. It was a woman with long hair. He tried to forget about it. It was late at night, after all. People see things in the dark. But every time he looked, he saw her silhouetted by the moon. She was pacing back and forth in front of arched windows. Even though he was embarrassed, he called the MacCallum police."

"Another one?" the police joked. Someone at the hotel called us last month about a woman in the tower.

After teasing him for a few minutes, the dispatcher agreed to send two officers to check it out.

The manager waited for them to check out the tower. Minutes passed. Then an hour. By the time they returned, he was about to call the police department for backup.

"I will tell you what happened," the policewoman said, "but only if you *never* speak of this again. Understand?"

The manager nodded.

"We went to the tower and knocked on the door," she said.

"We didn't hear a thing," said her partner. "Not a sound."

"Open up," the policewoman called through the door. "We need to make sure you're not in danger."

Silence.

The two took a step back and rammed their shoulders into the door.

Oddly, the door swung open the moment they made contact. The officers tumbled over each other into the room.

The policewoman struggled to her feet and held out her hand for her partner.

"That's the last time I answer a call about a ghost in the tower," he grumbled as he got to his feet.

But then, the door slammed shut. The lights dimmed and a cold fog covered them.

The policewoman's mouth dropped. As she watched, her partner was lifted into the air then *slammed* against a wall. How could that be? They were the only ones in the room.

Suddenly, something plucked her pistol from its holster and sent it flying through a window!

Shaken, she carefully leaned over the shattered window. Her pistol lay on the ground below the tower. She sighed and leaned back inside, but not before she noticed something odd. A few strands of long black hair lay on the window ledge.

How long had the hair been there? She understood how others might not have seen them. The clump was three or four strands, no more.

"Look what I have," she said to her partner, holding up the hair. "This is enough to keep a trace of the spirit who died here."

Her partner looked confused.

"I guess you haven't heard too many ghost stories," the officer said. "If someone dies a violent death, a part of their spirit is left behind." She laid the clump of hair back on the windowsill. "Give me your lighter."

Before he could toss it to her, a woman's raspy voice hissed from behind them. "*Give me that*!"

The two officers couldn't see her, but they heard every word. As the policeman looked in the direction of the voice, red scratches appeared on his arms, as if they'd been scratched with long fingernails. The lighter landed on the floor.

The policewoman was fast. She snatched the lighter and flicked it open. A small flame set the strands of hair on fire. The shadow of a woman appeared on the wall, even though no one was there. The shadow grew in size until its head grazed the ceiling. Then, for a brief moment, a figure materialized out of thin air, her face twisting with rage.

"Give me that!" the ghost roared.

But the flame had consumed the last thread of hair. The shadow disappeared, the cold fog dissipated, and the police were left standing in an empty room that smelled of burning rubber.

"We will never speak of this again," the policewoman said to her partner.

He agreed.

"I looked at the police reports that night," the clerk says. "It only mentioned a call to investigate something mysterious at the hotel. It never reported a ghost encounter."

"Why not?" you ask.

"Well." The clerk shrugs. "I guess they didn't think anyone would believe them."

A little while later, just before you go to sleep, you pull out your notebook. You make sure to write down everything the clerk said so you don't forget

one single detail. After all, the police might have promised never to speak about the ghost of the Casa de Palmas Hotel again . . .

. . . but *you* definitely didn't.

CHAPTER 8

Estero Llano Grande State Park

You're standing at the trailhead of Estero Llano Grande State Park. It's early morning, the best time for birding, your parents say. You don't mind, though, because it *also* happens to be a perfect time for ghost hunting. Morning, noon, or night, you know there are sure to be ghosts wandering the park's haunted paths.

That's what happens in a place where there's been a terrible tragedy.

It was here, back in December 1859, that the Texas Rangers killed every last man from the Tampacua people. Indigenous peoples had lived in this spot for over eleven thousand years. The land had plenty of game, and the lakes and rivers abounded with fish. Perhaps it's no wonder that when the Spanish soldiers, and then European settlers, saw it, they wanted it, too.

You picture the last battle in your head. The neighing of war horses, the glint of sword blades, cannonballs whizzing through the air, the cracks of muskets and rifles. You decide carefully where you want to go. You don't want to step in the wrong place. You might disturb a rattler. Or worse—a warrior spirit!

You've read enough history to know that when the Texas Rangers battled, they didn't give the defeated warriors the traditional burials of their people. So, where did their spirits go? If they weren't

buried according to ritual, they'd be destined to roam the earth forever.

Out of nowhere, there's a rustle in the bushes in front of you. From the corner of your eye, you see a white band—a bobcat's tail! This cat is only a bit bigger than a housecat, but much meaner. You glance around nervously, wondering where your parents are. It's not that you're scared. You've already battled plenty of paranormal pests, from human bundles, to deathly owls, to bleeding warriors. But an angry Tampacuan spirit warrior?

Gulp.

That's one you might panic about if it suddenly crossed your path.

Carefully, you retrace your steps on the trail. Your park map says the trail is five miles long. Sooner or later, you'll have to find your way back to the parking lot.

Right??

You would have gone faster, but there are

thorny trees on the path that you're trying to avoid, so your pace slows.

Suddenly, screeches like rusty hinges fill the air. It's the chachalaca birds. They always startle you. So much noise from a pack of little birds. What are they running from? The bobcat, you decide, but you reach for your Swiss army knife, just in case. You're about to flick it open when you hear a new sound. It's not an animal. Time to hunker down and wait to see what's coming.

The mesquite trees are now shrouded in a haze, a wispy, gray ground fog. That's when you spot them: three men, crouching so silently, you almost mistake them for part of the forest landscape. Their bodies are covered with tattoos. One has an ink alligator along his forearm. The others' arms are covered with jaguar spots.

Your heart hammers in your chest.

This is exactly what you were afraid of.

But just when you're sure it's your last minute

on earth, you pick up another sound: about twenty feet behind you, hard-soled boots crunch on the trail. When you see the wide-brimmed cowboy hat, you breathe a sigh of relief. It's a park ranger. It's not a real Texas Ranger, though; this man hasn't walked the earth for over a hundred years.

He and the Tampacuan men . . . are ghosts.

The Ranger raises his rifle, the Tampacuans lift their knives.

You squeeze your eyes shut, bracing for the worst. But—nothing happens.

When you open them again, you realize none of the ghosts are looking at you. In fact, it's almost like they don't see you at all. Instead, their eyes are locked firmly upon one another. As if they are fated to replay this last battle again and again, until the end of time.

You slip your Swiss Army knife back into your pocket and creep slowly out of the way. If they're going to battle each other, you'd rather not be right in the middle.

Ahead, through the thorn trees, you see car lights flashing on and off. That's your mom and dad's signal for you to find them.

They call your name. Your mom's voice is high-pitched, and your dad's sentences end in little squeaks. They're scared. Maybe they saw the bobcat? They weren't with you to see the ghosts. How scared could they be?

When your parents call your name a second time, you've already made it back to the parking lot.

CHAPTER 9

The Shary Mansion

You've had your fill of scary ghosts. So this evening, you're going to visit a nice one.

At least, that's what your parents promised. After your experience at the Colonial Hotel and in the Estero Llano Grande State Park, you all need a happy encounter.

In life, his name was John Harry Shary. He established the first large-scale commercial citrus orchard in the Rio Grande Valley and eventually became known as "Father of the Texas Citrus Industry." While some ghosts hang around a place because of bad blood or unfinished business, in this case, many believe the opposite is true: John Shary simply loved his home *so* much, he never wanted to leave.

When you pull up to the mansion at sundown, you can see why.

The Shary Mansion definitely seems like the kind of place a "good mood" ghost would haunt. Big enough for a ballroom and a bowling alley, nestled amid groves of grapefruit trees and sitting on the shores of a three-acre lake, the mansion *has* to be more fun than a tomb, no matter how pretty it is. The chapel seems a pleasant place, you have to admit. A steepled building of sandy-colored bricks, the mausoleum towers over the trees.

"So many people have seen the Shary ghost," your mom says, "that they've stopped keeping count. Especially in the evening, when he crosses the road from the cemetery back to the house."

"Has he always haunted the mansion?" you ask.

"Not until the Shary family sold it," your mom says. "After John Shary died, his adopted daughter and husband took over. The house seemed to have a life of its own. Texas Governor Allan Shivers and President Dwight David Eisenhower spent time there. All the ghostly reports began after the new owner, a businessman, started renovations and repairs. The businessman wanted to turn the house into a gathering place for intellectuals, businessmen, and artists." She pauses. "That's when Mr. Shary appeared."

"Ahh," you sigh as you stretch out on the car blanket. "No grasping hands, no demon coachman—just a spirit who won't leave?"

Your mom nods. "They say he adored his magnolia trees. And he had *another* good reason to stay . . . "

But before she can finish her sentence, she gasps. Her mouth opens and shuts like a goldfish in a bowl. It seems as if the lake mist has lifted and moved to cover the chapel. The mist shifts, then coalesces into a single figure. Although made of haze, there's no question what the spirit is.

Or *who*.

Dressed in a tuxedo and round glasses, the ghost of John Shary stands still for a moment, then disappears. He reappears a few seconds later on the steps leading up to the mansion. You can see his wispy form settle on a rocking chair on the porch.

Rock, rock . . . pause. *Rock, rock* . . . pause.

You can't believe you're watching a ghost in a rocking chair.

After a few minutes, Mr. Shary stands up and looks around the porch as if he's expecting someone. Suddenly, he smiles, though you aren't sure why. Then he steps off the porch and disappears around the corner of the house. You follow

Mr. Shary, just in time to see him standing over the lake. He hovers a few feet above the water, just high enough so his shoes don't get wet. He holds out his hand like a gentleman does when he asks someone to dance.

Your mom sneezes.

"*Shh*," you and your dad chorus. Your mom pinches her nose. "I think I'm allergic to something here."

Whatever it is is lovely, but it almost makes you sneeze, too. You aren't used to the deeply sweet scent in the air. Floral, like roses, but with a touch of citrus.

What is that, anyway? Some kind of flower?

"Look!" Your dad motions excitedly toward the lake. "Hurry! You might miss it!"

You rush over and gasp, elated. This was what you came to see. A ghostly woman, her arms placed on his shoulders, sways along with Mr. Shary, as if to some music only they can hear. Her dress floats, cloudlike, as they dance across the sky.

Your parents sigh. "Isn't it romantic?" your dad says.

You nod, but then you sneeze.

Jeez. What's with all the sneezing?!

Suddenly, you realize you must have been watching them all night. The sky lightens as you watch. Finally, the darkness thins, revealing a pale pink sky, and the two figures fade away into the light.

As you head toward the car, you can't help

noticing a deep sense of calm pass over you. One last time, you glance back at the Shary Mansion. With all its elegance and warmth, you can see why Mr. Shary loved it so much.

"Look!" your mom cries when the three of you reach the car. There, laying neatly across the hood, is a beautiful bouquet of magnolias.

"*Achoo!*" you all sneeze in unison. You look at each other. And then, you laugh.

Magnolias.

Mr. Shary's favorite flower.

CHAPTER 10

The LaBorde House

Your parents say you have too much imagination. They think that's why you see so many ghosts. You, on the other hand, say a creative mind is the best way to learn new things.

So, when your family steps into the LaBorde House, you smile. You don't even have to close your eyes to picture yourself back in the early 1900s. The heavy Victorian furniture, the ornate wrought iron balcony, and, behind a closed door, underground tunnels, some of which led to nowhere. It takes you right back to the past.

"The Red Room?" The clerk asks. "It's available. You're lucky, everyone wants to stay there."

Your parents look at each other and shrug. Why not?

"Let's see why it's so popular," your mom says.

As your parents squeeze a rollaway bed into the room, you step outside. You look over the balcony, down to the courtyard. You wonder who has stayed in the room before you.

You imagine guests like cattle ranchers who had just sold a herd on the Rio Grande River dock. Military men who stopped by on their way to new posts. Riverboat passengers who wanted to spend a night onshore.

The clerk tells you that LaBorde has not just one, but a number of haunted rooms and haunted tunnels underneath it. It has a reputation that everyone in South Texas knows about. The entire building is said to be full of full-body apparitions, mysterious footsteps, and ghostly physical contact. A ghost touching you? You can't wait.

How can a seventeen-room hotel hold so many ghosts? Your mom is the one to tell the story this time.

"It all started with a romance gone wrong. A young army lieutenant fell in love with one of the hotel residents. The Lady in Red, the locals called her. Maybe it was because her room was decorated in shades of red. Maybe it was the way she dressed, also always in red. Or perhaps it was her perfume. She always smelled of freshly cut roses.

The Lady in Red gave up her other suitors and dedicated herself to the soldier. He'd promised to marry her and begin a life together in a new city. He was faithful, for a time. But one afternoon, he didn't come back. The Lady in Red, alarmed, traveled to the soldier's

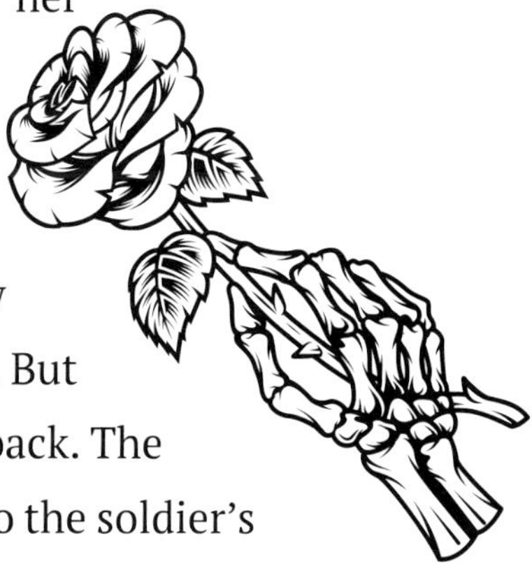

fort. Was he ill? Injured? Can you imagine how she felt when she realized he had deserted her?"

"Even worse," your dad adds, "when she found out he had gone home to marry someone else."

"People said the news shattered her," your mom continues. "She refused to leave her room. The other guests heard her wails all the way into the courtyard. But one night, the crying stopped. The Lady in Red had opened the door to her balcony and jumped. The townsfolk shook their heads and said she should have known better than to trust a soldier.

Hers wasn't the only death here, though. The townspeople had more sympathy for the two little girls who died here next. They had come to the hotel for a health cure. No one knows which one was sick. Maybe they both were. At that time, underground springs were considered a wonderful health treatment. Some claimed underground springs could cure anything. That's what brought the girls to the LaBorde House—its deep cistern of spring water.

One day, though, something terrible happened. The girls fell into the well. Had one died while trying to rescue the other? Had they both fallen at the same time? You think about it the rest of the day and as you fall asleep that night. The image of

the drowning haunts your dreams . . . until a racket next door wakes you.

The people in the room next door are chasing each other and having a good time doing so. The high-pitched yips and giggles threaten to burst through the wall.

Your parents are sleeping, so you decide to take care of the problem. You stomp to the front desk and ring the bell. You ask the manager to quiet the noisy family.

He takes a step back, looking amazed. "You're joking, right?"

You convince him you're serious.

He pulls up the hotel register on the computer, then swivels the screen for you to see. There aren't any guests registered next door.

"You've heard the story about the girls that drowned in the cistern?" he asks.

You nod.

"Your room is next to theirs." He shrugs.

"Usually, people want paranormal activity. That's why they come here."

Of course. It was ghosts. You mumble a "thank you," and go back to bed only to be awoken a little while later.

Thump!

You hear footsteps in the hall.

Thump. Thump!

The footsteps speed up and pass by your door, only to return a few seconds later. Is it the soldier, trying to say "sorry" to the Lady in Red?

The doorknob rattles. You try to shut your eyes, but now you're a little spooked. You're not sure how long you lay there, body taut and ready to run.

Somehow, the time passes. The rising sun sends shafts of light through the window onto the oriental rug. That's the moment you smell roses. The sweet, spicy scent is nothing like the magnolias you smelled at the Shary Mansion.

This scent is heavy. *Too* heavy. You feel like it will smother you.

"Wake up, something's wrong!" You jump out of bed and open the balcony door so you can breathe the fresh air from outside.

To your surprise, you see that the tunnel door across the courtyard, previously closed, is open. No one would mind if you had a peek. Tunnels that don't lead anywhere? You have to see it.

People said the Chicago mobster Al Capone smuggled alcohol from Mexico all the way to speakeasy bars in America, by way of Roma, Texas. At that time, selling and drinking alcohol was against the law. Some thought Al Capone or his henchmen still roamed the tunnels.

However, when you descend the stairs, you don't hear clanking bottles. You hear the clanking of . . . chains? *Clink, clank, shuffle* . . . then, was that a sigh of distress? You peek around the corner to see a family of three hiding in the shadows.

They seem to sense you are there. They turn toward you and hold up their chains. It's almost as if they are asking for help.

You wonder, how could they walk? They are all so thin and weak. They have hollows in their cheeks and smudges of exhaustion under their eyes.

Suddenly, you realize they are ghosts of people who tried to escape enslavement. Had these tunnels led some to freedom, or had the twists and turns tricked them to a terrible end?

You have to leave. Not because you are afraid, but because you feel you might cry.

You trudge up the stairs and climb back into bed. Ghost hunting is different than you expected. You had no idea it could make you so sad.

CHAPTER 11

The Woman in White at Roma

You sit on a park bench outside the church parish hall in Roma, Texas. The sun beats down, but in the shade of the ebony trees, you're comfortable.

Once again, you're blanketed in the scent of flowers. Thank goodness, the ebony flowers don't smell like the roses at LaBorde Hotel. This smell is musky, a bit heavy, but not overpowering.

"Not much to see here," you tell yourself as you open one of your books.

A broody hen squawks somewhere close by. The sharp squawking startles you and you drop your book.

A young couple stroll by, arm in arm.

"Are you okay?" the young woman asks you.

"Those chickens could raise the dead," her boyfriend says. "They see a cat or fox and warn the whole brood."

"Not all ghosts need to be awakened," the young woman says. "There's one spirit here who never sleeps."

You pick up your notebook, click your pen, and say, "Will you tell me more?"

"Everyone should know the story of Isabel," said the boyfriend.

"I'll start by telling you something about our town, Roma," the young woman says. "Many of our families are faithful Catholics. If one of the children choses a life dedicated to God, everyone is proud. So, when Isabel, one of the local girls, said she wanted to become a nun, her family took her to the convent to meet with the Mother Superior.

The Mother Superior, gifted with an understanding of people, told Isabel to wait six months before taking her vows as a nun. That would give Isabel time to think about her choice.

Isabel agreed. She knew she was ready, but more time would just make her choice clearer, she thought. During that time, she did her home chores and community service, but she also spent some time in partial seclusion at the convent. She counted down the days until she could become a nun.

But then she met Daniel. She'd been sweeping the convent porch when she felt someone staring at her. Isabel whipped around, holding the broom in front of her. "Who are you and why are you looking at me like that?"

Daniel laughed and apologized. He explained that he was new in town and hoped someone like her would show him around Roma.

Isabel was an innocent girl, but she wasn't foolish. She kept her distance but answered his questions about life in Roma.

Daniel was funny. After a while, Isabel relaxed. Talking to him was a harmless, fun way to spend time.

Isabel's family noticed Daniel when he attended mass at the church. He'd look for Isabel among the worshippers. When he saw her, he'd nod respectfully to her and her family. After a time, they accepted Daniel as a good man and happily joined in the wedding preparations when Isabel announced she wanted to marry him.

Isabel was an only child, and her parents wanted the day to be special. Weeks were spent sewing her wedding dress. Every stitch was perfect.

Meanwhile, across the world, trouble brewed. In Spain, a group fought against the king, wanting independence. Young men, perhaps seeking adventure, or genuinely interested in freedom for the Spanish people, made their way to Spain. A brigade of men from the United States and Mexico named themselves the Abraham Lincoln Battalion and went to fight.

Daniel was one of those young men.

No one wanted Daniel to go. It was only when Daniel promised he would return in time for the wedding that Isabel gave her permission for him to leave. Months later, though, Daniel's regiment was wiped out in a battle. Two-thirds of the men lost their lives. Daniel was one of them.

Isabel refused to believe Daniel was dead. How could he be? They had planned out their life together, one with children and joy. It wasn't possible that he was gone.

Not a night went by that Isabel didn't walk the plaza looking for Daniel. Each night, she'd put on her wedding dress. Her family begged her not to do it, but there was no stopping her. Eventually, Isabel's dress tore and shredded. The white lace became stained with mud. She frightened people when she'd push her way into a crowd and asked if they had seen Daniel.

After a time, Isabel's nightly wandering killed her. She never stopped searching for Daniel out in the cold, in the rain. She became sick and died.

The young woman sighs. "Isabel used to sit on this bench, everyone says so. Some people say they *still* see Isabel and Daniel sitting here, laughing and talking like they must have done when they were alive." She smiles at her boyfriend and squeezes his hand.

This bench? You stand up, sit down, and stand back up.

"Go look in the plaza," the young woman says. "Maybe you'll see the woman in white."

You walk to the plaza and look for a woman in a wedding dress but don't find her. By the time you return to the bench, the young couple has vanished. That's too bad, you think. You wanted to ask them more questions about the lady in white.

Suddenly, you notice something stuck in one of the ebony branches overhead. That's funny. You don't remember seeing anything there before.

You reach up and pull it out, careful not to scratch yourself.

When you open your hand, you realize it's the tattered remnant of a white lace wedding dress.

A Ghostly Goodbye

You're sorry when it's time to leave the Rio Grande Valley. Your mom and dad want to come back soon. They read about South Padre Island and want to visit there next. It's the best birding location in the western hemisphere. You wouldn't mind seeing an alligator or two.

You'd like to come back and taste more Rio Grande Valley food. Pickle-flavored ice and red pepper hot chocolate. Who knew they could be so good? You've never been to a place where you can see weather coming, or where someone's ranch is bigger than a state.

As for ghosts . . . Have you had physical contact with spirits? *Check*. Full body apparitions? *Check*. Mysterious footsteps and smells from the great beyond? *Check and check.*

When your car crosses the state line, you all say, “We’ll be back!” at the same time.

Then you pop a churro into your mouth and smile.

Karen Emily Miller has been writing about strange creatures since she was six years old, so writing about the paranormal is a perfect fit. She just moved to Iowa City and is excited to meet new ghosts there.

Check out some of the other *Spooky America* titles available now!

Spooky America was adapted from the creeptastic *Haunted America* series for adults. *Haunted America* explores historical haunts in cities and regions across America. Here's more from the original *Ghosts of the Rio Grande Valley* author, David Bowles:

www.davidbowles.us